by Dean John Ireland in 1827, but this was lost in the last war. In 1841 Thomas Ward and J.H.Nixon won the competition to supply glass for the south rose and the lancets below it, as the previous glass had disappeared, with subjects illustrating the Old Testament and the miracles and life of Christ. They also provided some of the glass for an ambitious scheme of glazing in the clerestory (upper) windows in the nave and transepts during the 1850s and 60s depicting angels and prophets. None of this rather dark glass now remains as the south rose was re-glazed in 1902 and what remained of the clerestory glass was removed after the Second World War. In 1860 the first of the memorial windows were inserted. The lancets below the north rose and one in the west aisle of the north transept commemorated officers killed in the Indian Mutiny of 1857 but this did not survive the war. Also at this time the first memorial windows to eminent engineers were introduced. Those to Robert Stephenson, Isambard Kingdom Brunel and Richard Trevithick still survive but those to Joseph Locke (1805–60) and Sir Charles William Siemens (1823–83) were removed in order to facilitate a new glazing scheme in the nave. Locke's window was removed to Barnsley and fragments from the Siemens window were used in the 1950s in the rebuilt Lantern. Victorian windows to composer Vincent Novello, poet Geoffrey Chaucer, Lady Augusta Stanley (wife of the eminent Dean Arthur Stanley) and men who died in the Ashanti War in West Africa in 1873–4 were also victims of blast damage during the war, as were the "St Edward" window in the south transept given by James Hora in memory of his wife in 1903, and the window to members of the Queen's Westminster Rifles who died in the First World War.

In 1907 Dean Armitage Robinson and Scottish-born architect J.Ninian Comper drew up a major scheme for the windows in the north aisle of the nave, when it was decided that each one should include large figures of a king of England and an abbot of Westminster from the same period, in whose reign building work was carried on at the Abbey. Each forms a memorial to an eminent engineer. Comper took great pains with his designs and especially arranged for the glassmakers, Messrs Chance, to use earthenware rather than steel crucibles to mix the cobalt oxide in order to reproduce the purity of his blue colours in the medieval tradition. Hugh Easton was commissioned to replace much of the glass destroyed during the Second World War. His work includes memorials to nurses, Battle of Britain pilots and citizens of Westminster who lost their lives in the conflict. The major additions of the late 20th century were the series in the Lady Chapel recording benefactors to the Abbey's restoration appeal (1973–1995), and a window to commemorate poets and writers. What follows is a description of the windows to be seen in the Abbey today, commencing at the main north entrance.

BELOW North rose window

BOTTOM North lancet windows

FACING PAGE Bunyan window detail

1 NORTH ROSE WINDOW

Designed by Sir James Thornhill (1675–1734) ◆ **Glass installed 1722**

The stonework of the rose was altered in 1722 and Dean Atterbury decided to fill it with stained glass. The designer's full-size cartoons for the figures in this window still survive in Chinnor Church, Oxfordshire. Sixteen seven-foot figures of Christ, the Apostles (except Judas Iscariot) and the four Evangelists were executed by glass painter Joshua Price. In the centre circle is the Bible inscribed with the Greek words meaning "Word of the Cross". The glass was altered and slightly rearranged by the Abbey's architect J.L.Pearson when he restored the north front in the late 19th century and the feet of some of the figures were cut off. The glass in the rose was boarded over during the Second World War and escaped bomb damage.

SIX LANCETS BELOW THE ROSE

Designed by Brian Thomas (1912–1989) ◆ **Installed 1958**

This design replaced the war-damaged Indian Mutiny memorial windows. The scenes depict six acts of mercy from St Matthew's gospel (ie. feeding the hungry, giving drink to the thirsty, clothing the naked, harbouring the stranger, visiting the sick and ministering to prisoners). Designed to

harmonise with the older rose window above it, the glass was made at Whitefriars Studio by James Powell and Sons and is of a type known technically as seedy glass, being deliberately filled with tiny bubbles. The thickset peasant figures are portrayed in a brown monochrome but the colours in the design range from bright crimson to vivid blue-green.

2 JOHN BUNYAN (1628–1688)
Designed by J.Ninian Comper (1864–1960) ◆ Dedicated 25 January 1912

Erected by public subscription, this window in the west aisle commemorates the author of *The Pilgrim's Progress* and shows eight scenes from the first part of this book, commencing with a portrait of Bunyan asleep and dreaming in the lower left panel. Following from the bottom of each light in an ascending line the large pictures show: Christian and the Evangelist in the fields; Goodwill receiving Christian at the wicket gate; Christian seeing the Crucifixion; Piety, Prudence and Charity arming Christian; (next light) the fight with Apollyon; Christian and Faithful in Vanity Fair; Christian and Hopeful meeting the two shining men after crossing the river; Christian and Hopeful entering the gate of the City. The tracery at the top shows the vision of the Lamb and the ringing of bells in the Celestial City. The inscription reads: "In memory of John Bunyan. The Pilgrim's Progress. B.1628. D.1688"

3 HMS CAPTAIN
Designed by J.R.Clayton and Alfred Bell ◆ Installed 1871

This ship went down off Cape Finisterre on 7 September 1870 with the loss of all the crew. It was an experimental design and unfortunately did not withstand a moderate gale. The scenes shown are from the Old and New Testaments, (left from the top): building the Ark, the passage through the Red Sea, Solomon's fleet of ships, building the ship of Tyre and Jonah's deliverance from the whale, (right): Christ stilling the tempest, walking on the water, teaching from the ship, the miracle of the draught of fishes and St Paul's shipwreck. A brass on the floor below the window commemorates Captain Hugh Burgoyne V.C., Captain Cowper Coles and the officers, men and boys who died.

From the west:

4 BRITISH PRISONERS OF WAR 1914–18
Designed by J.Ninian Comper ◆ Dedicated 14 June 1926

This window is part of the Comper series, commenced in the nave, and depicts King Henry VI (d.1471) and Richard Harweden, Abbot of Westminster. The scene above the King's figure shows him asleep as a prisoner in the Tower of London, after he was deposed. Above the Abbot the scene shows the King pointing out the place for his tomb beside the shrine of Edward the Confessor in the Abbey, but actually Henry was buried at Windsor. At the head of the window is a cinquefoil containing the red rose of the House of Lancaster and various shields connected with the King. Small statuettes in the design represent members of Henry VI's family and the words *Dieu et mon Droit* (God and my right), which Henry was the first to assume as a regular royal motto, also appear. The window was given by James Gerard, United States Ambassador in charge of British interests in Berlin and the inscription reads: "In memory of British Prisoners who died in Germany 1914–1918. A tribute from the American Ambassador in Berlin 1914–1917". The coat of arms of the United States appears at the base with those of the United Kingdom and Commonwealth countries.

5 JAMES TURLE (1802–1882)
Designed by Clayton and Bell

Turle was organist of the Abbey from 1831–1882. The design shows figures of various Biblical characters including David, Miriam, Jubal, Asaph, Deborah and Moses, and the Virgin Mary with saints Ambrose, Bretinus and Cecilia. Small portraits of Turle and his wife Mary occur at the base of the window, slightly obscured by the monuments on the window sill. Turle has a memorial tablet in the cloisters but is buried in Norwood cemetery.

6 ROBERT STEPHENSON (1803–1859)
Designed by William Wailes (1809–1881) (amended by Sir George Gilbert Scott) ◆ Installed 1862

This was originally in the nave, where Stephenson is buried. The order of the medallions was changed when it was moved to this position in 1934 and plain white glass was substituted for the coloured background to let in more light. The portrait heads of famous engineers in the top cinquefoil are of his father George, Thomas Telford, John Smeaton, Robert himself, James Watt and John Rennie. A depiction of Robert's bridge over the Nile and the Victoria bridge over the St Lawrence river in Canada are shown at the top of each light with the high level bridge at

Newcastle-upon-Tyne and the Britannia railway bridge over the Menai Straits at the base. The other medallions between depict Biblical building, alternating with smaller heads of famous builders of history: (left) Tubal Cain, building the Ark, Noah, erection of the Tabernacle, Hiram, Solomon's temple, Bezaleel, building the second Temple, and William Wykeham; (right) Cheops, building of Nineveh, Euclid, cities of Egypt, Archimedes, a Roman aqueduct, Michaelangelo, the Colosseum and Sir Christopher Wren. In 1948 a representation of the famous "Rocket" locomotive was added at the bottom of the window to commemorate Robert's father. The inscription at the base of the window was also altered and now reads: "Robert Stephenson MP, DCL, FRS 1803–1859 President of the Institution of Civil Engineers son of George Stephenson 1781–1848 Father of Railways".

FAR LEFT Stephenson window detail

RIGHT The Prisoners of War window

7 ISLIP CHAPEL – UPPER CHANTRY, THE NURSES' MEMORIAL

Designed by Hugh Easton (1906–1965) ◆ Dedicated 2 November 1950

This chantry, originally built by Abbot John Islip (d.1532), was newly furnished and dedicated as the Nurses' Memorial Chapel by the late Queen Elizabeth The Queen Mother, to commemorate the nurses and midwives from the Commonwealth who died during the 1939–45 war. A Roll of Honour is kept in the chapel. The subject of the window is a representation of Our Lady standing on the crescent moon carrying the Christ Child who blesses the figure of a uniformed nurse kneeling below. Behind the Virgin's head is the golden sun and the star of Bethlehem shines down from above. Shown above the nurse is St Luke, the beloved physician, standing on a rainbow. In the tracery at the very top is the lamp of Florence Nightingale placed on a Red Cross surrounded by a crown of thorns. At the base are shown badges of the nursing services, with the names and coats of arms of all the countries from which nurses came to serve in the war. The cockerel device used by Easton and the names of his assistants also appear. This small chapel is not open to general visitors but application to view can be made to a Verger at the Abbey and services of Holy Communion are often held here.

ISLIP CHAPEL – LOWER CHANTRY

Designed by Hugh Easton ◆ Dedicated 13 March 1948

This was the gift of Alan Don, Dean of Westminster, as a thank-offering for the safe deliverance of the Abbey and St Margaret's Church Westminster from the perils of war. The figures are of Abbot Islip, builder of this chapel, and St Margaret of Antioch transfixing an evil dragon with the Cross of Christ. Incorporated in the window is a diamond-shaped piece of medieval glass showing the rebus of the Abbot – an eye and a man slipping from a tree, being a pun on his name I-slip. Cherubs hold small models of the Abbey (with flames coming from the central area which received damage in 1941) and St Margaret's. The coats of arms of Paul de Labilliere, Dean during the war years, and Dean Don, sometime Rector of St Margaret's, also appear. This window can be viewed through the chapel screen.

8 HENRY V CHANTRY CHAPEL - FOUR KINGS
Designed by Edward Woore ◆ Installed 1952

This small four-light window can just be seen above the altar in this chantry. The four kings represented, with their coats of arms below, are all buried in the Abbey: Henry III, Edward III, Henry V and Henry VII. The designer used glass made by Burlison and Grylls, salvaged from a war-damaged window in the south transept. A window installed by Dean Ireland was originally in this position.

FACING PAGE TOP
The Nurses' Memorial Chapel

FACING PAGE BOTTOM
John Islip's rebus

BELOW The four-light window above Henry V Chantry altar

9 WEST WINDOW

Designed by John Lawson (of Goddard & Gibbs)
◆ **Unveiled 19 October 1995.**

The unveiling of this large window by Her Majesty The Queen marked the culmination of a 22-year programme of Abbey restoration. It contains initials, cyphers and coats of arms of generous donors to the Westminster Abbey Trust's appeal and those connected with fundraising. It particularly honours Sir John Templeton (b.1912), a major benefactor. The lines from Psalm 26 read "Lord, I have loved the habitation of thy house" beside the panel containing the Templeton arms. The arms of the Sovereign appear in the centre section, flanked on the south by the heraldic achievement of the Duke of Edinburgh (Chairman of the Westminster Abbey Trust), with the small shield of Henry VII on the right, and on the north by the arms of Charles, Prince of Wales (Grand Master of the Most Honourable Order of the Bath), with the small shield of Elizabeth of York, wife of Henry VII, to the left. Directly above the Queen's achievement are the coats of arms of three deans of Westminster (from the left) Eric Abbott, Michael Mayne and Edward Carpenter, flanked in the single lights by Lord Blake (left) and Lord Weatherill, former High Steward and High Bailiff of Westminster respectively. In the top five lights can be seen the emblem of St Margaret of Antioch, the cross and martlets of Edward the Confessor, the lilies of Our Lady, the arms of the monastery of Westminster, the crossed keys of St Peter and the emblem of St Faith. The coats of arms along the bottom of the window are mostly those of Trustees, (from the left) Sir John Davis; Lord Sainsbury (top) and Sir Eric Drake; Lord Catto and Lord Errol of Hale; Lord Rupert Nevill and Sir Denis Mountain; Canon Colin Semper; Sir Reginald Pullen and J.Peter Foster (Surveyor); Garfield Weston (initials); Sir John Templeton; Helen Walton; Rear Admiral Kenneth Snow and Donald Buttress; Sir Peter Walters; the firm of Mowlem (contractors) and Sir Philip Harris; the Duke of Westminster and Lord Robens; Hugh Ridley Sykes and Sir Anthony Tuke; and Herbert Ryle (Dean 1911–25). The window was devised by Donald Buttress, the Abbey Surveyor, with Hubert Chesshyre of the College of Arms. The design of the window reflects the colourful heraldry to be found on the banners of Knights of the Order of the Bath which hang in this chapel.

10 CENTRAL EAST WINDOW

Designed by Alan Younger ◆ **Dedicated 22 November 2000**

This new window celebrates the Blessed Virgin Mary. In the centre is the Assumption with angels who hold scrolls inscribed with the first verses of the Magnificat. In the lower panels is a Nativity scene with the shepherds and wise men. The star of Bethlehem is depicted as the Hale Bopp comet, which was passing over the designer's home as he was working on the window. On either side of the Nativity is the Annunciation with the angel Gabriel, and the Virgin at prayer. At the base can be seen the coat of arms and kneeling figures of the donors of this window Lord and Lady Harris of Peckham wearing academic gowns.

11 DONOR WINDOWS IN THE APSIDAL CHAPELS

Designed by Alfred Fisher and Peter Archer
◆ **Installed 1995 and 1997**

Small windows also commemorate major donors to the restoration appeal, many of them from the United States of America. From the north side, following around the chapel the names are: Gordon and Jean Southam, Williams/Wogen, Templeton Gargiulo, Vella Templeton, John Zochonis, Derek Crowson, Hugh Ridley Sykes, Leopold Muller, Governor and Mrs James Noe senior, Linda and Christel Noe Laine (also known as the "Louisiana window"), L.J. and Mary Skaggs (who have two panels), Lord Catto, Stanley Ho, Walter Annenberg, John Latsis, M. & J. Sackler and family, the Duke of Westminster, Lucina Ho, Lord Robens and Sir Harry Djanogly.

12 BATTLE OF BRITAIN MEMORIAL

Designed by Hugh Easton
◆ **Dedicated 10 July 1947**

The easternmost chapel was newly furnished after the war as the Royal Air Force Chapel and unveiled by King George VI. The magnificent 48-light window commemorates fighter pilots and crew who died during the Battle of Britain from July to October 1940. In the upper tier are the heavenly Seraphim with six wings in brilliant blue-and wine- coloured glass with hands outstretched to Paradise. The lower lights contain the badges of the fighter squadrons that took part in the battle. In four panels are shown visions symbolising the Redemption. In the upper left a Squadron Leader kneels before the Virgin and the Christ Child. Below she is shown holding the dead Christ in her arms as a symbol of the sacrifice of the mothers and widows of those who fell in the battle. A Flying Officer is shown kneeling here. On the opposite side is a Sergeant Pilot bowing his head before a vision of the Crucifixion, symbolising the sacrifice of the pilot himself, and a Pilot Officer witnesses a vision of the Resurrection, symbolising the pilot's triumph. In the centre panels can be seen the Royal arms and the badge of the Royal Air Force with the motto *Per ardua ad astra* (Through struggle to the stars), together with the badge of the Fleet Air Arm and the furled flags of New Zealand,

The Battle of Britain Window

Upper register:

421 FLIGHT 248 422 FLIGHT	THE INCARNATION	ROYAL ARMS FLEET AIR ARM	THE FLAGS OF N.Z. CANADA AUSTRALIA SOUTH AFRICA	THE FLAGS OF CZECH. POLAND BELGIUM U.S.A.	ROYAL AIR FORCE 3	THE RESURRECTION	235 FIGHTER INTER-CEPTOR UNIT
		232	247	263	245		236

Middle register:

1 17	THE PIETA	610 616	504 600	THE CRUCIFIXION	253 401 RCAF
19 23		607 605	611 602		303 POLAND 310
32 43		609 615	604 603		501 302 POLAND

Lower register:

41 64	74 72	85 87	213 141	219 242	249 601
25 29	56 65	79 111	145 151	234 238	266 312
54 46	66 73	92	152	229 222	264 257

Canada, Australia, South Africa, Czechoslovakia, Poland, Belgium and the United States of America. Representatives of all these countries, as well as other Commonwealth nations, fought with British pilots in the battle. There are now 70 squadron badges in the window, some which were inadvertently left out of the original design having been added in 1961. Throughout the background of the design flows a rose tree, the rose of England having been a badge of Henry VII, and the branches intertwine around the squadron badges. At the bottom of the window are the words "We few, we happy few, we band of brothers" from Shakespeare's *Henry V*. The names of the leaders of the RAF during the war were painted on the stonework beneath the window in 1989 and Air Chief Marshal Dowding, who led Fighter Command in 1940, is buried in the Chapel.

13 SIDE AISLES

The last pieces of Tudor glass in the chapel were blown out during the Second World War but some small quarries showing the crowned initials H and R (for Henricus Rex) from the lower east window were salvaged and set in the western windows of the side aisles. The curves of the letter 'h' are formed by small dragons. Some further salvaged fragments with the same design were set in the abstract windows of the east cloister.

FACING PAGE **Battle of Britain window**

BELOW **Walter Annenberg's window**

14 HERALDIC SHIELDS IN ST EDMUND'S CHAPEL

These three early specimens of heraldic glass, each about 16 inches in height, were placed in the window of this chapel in 1938, having been removed from the apse windows. They may originally have been set within the grisaille glass which adorned the church in the medieval period. Shields with these arms are recorded as being in the windows of this chapel in 1686 and it is possible Wren moved them up to the apse when he re-set the windows there. The heater-shaped shields show the three lions of England for Henry III, the red pallets of Provence for his queen Eleanor of Provence, and the red lion rampant crowned, in a border bezanty, for Richard, Earl of Cornwall (and King of the Romans), Henry's brother-in-law. Only Henry's shield is in its original state. Eleanor's arms have vine leaf decoration as a diaper pattern on the gold coloured glass, and there is much blue glass used to patch the Cornwall shield in the border, which should be black. (Carved shields of all three of these arms can be seen in the choir aisles.)

15 ST BENEDICT'S CHAPEL - CITIZENS OF WESTMINSTER

Designed by Hugh Easton and associates
◆ **Dedicated 7 November 1948**

This replaces a window to the Queen's Westminster Rifles which was blown out during the war. It shows St George and St Michael both slaying the dragon and symbolises the sacrifice of the citizens of the City of Westminster who died during the last war. It includes badges and emblems of the armed services, the Westminster Dragoons, Queen's Westminsters, the Home Guard, Police and Fire services, civil defence and voluntary services. The coat of arms of the City of Westminster granted by Elizabeth I in 1601 appears at the base, with supporters and crest granted by Queen Victoria. The inscription reads: "To the memory of those citizens of Westminster who gave their lives in the war of 1939–1945".

THE APSE AND LANTERN

16 APSE WINDOWS

These can best be viewed from the lantern area. From the north the figures are thought to depict Christ and Our Lady, St Edward the Confessor and St John the Evangelist (in the guise of a beggar), and St Augustine with Mellitus, Bishop of London. The figures of St Edward, except his head, and St John may date from around 1490. The name of the glazier, Edward Drew and the date 1706, appears in some of the glass, when these fragments were gathered together. They were all restored in the 1920s and were boarded over during the last war.

EAST WINDOW OF THE TRIFORIUM
Designed by J.Ninian Comper
◆ **Installed 1951**

Below the sets of figures in the apse can be seen a two-light window showing Queen Eleanor of Castile and Lady Margaret Beaufort (mother of Henry VII), who are both buried in the Abbey. The cost of this window, and that above Henry V's Chantry, was defrayed by John A. Dickins. The previous window here, to Archdeacon Bentinck, was blown out during the war.

17 LANTERN WINDOWS

This area was badly damaged by bombing on the night of 10/11 May 1941 and the roof fell in, destroying the Victorian glass. The windows of the newly-constructed lantern are filled with fragments of glass from various war-damaged windows.

ABOVE **Medieval heraldic shields**

LEFT **Citizens of Westminster window**

RIGHT **St Edward and the Pilgrim in the Apse**

18 SOUTH ROSE WINDOW
Devised by G.F. Bodley and M.R. James ◆ Dedicated 26 September 1902

This rose window is said to be the largest of its type, being approximately 32 feet across. The glass, painted by Messrs Burlison and Grylls, was given as a memorial to Hugh Lupus Grosvenor, 1st Duke of Westminster (1825–1899), replacing rather garish Victorian glass. In the centre is the figure of Christ, surrounded by 16 figures symbolical of the Virtues and Orders of Angels. In the outer circle are 32 figures chosen to represent the preparation of the world for Christ (these include 16 prophets and learned men such as Plato and Aristotle). The four small lights in the corners represent (from top left) Adam, St John the Baptist, Gabriel and the Blessed Virgin Mary.

The 12 lancets below the rose represent teachers of the Greek and Latin church (from the left): Saints Clement of Alexandria, Athanasius, Chrysostom, Jerome, Augustine of Hippo and Gregory the Great, with the arms of St Peter (crossed keys) and St Paul above, between the Royal arms. In the lower range Christianity in the British Isles is represented in the persons of (from left to right): Saints Alban, Ninian, Patrick, David, Augustine of Canterbury and Aidan. The arms above the lower figures are of St Edward the Confessor, the medieval Abbey, the City of Westminster, the Duke, the Dean and Chapter of Westminster and again the Royal arms.

FACING PAGE **South rose window**

ABOVE **The South Transept and its rose window**

BELOW **Detail from the Poets' window**

19 EDWARD HORTON HUBBARD / THE POETS' WINDOW
Designed by Graham Jones ◆ Dedicated 7 June 1994

This modern window above Geoffrey Chaucer's tomb in Poets' Corner is a memorial to Edward Horton Hubbard, who did much to save the Victorian heritage of Liverpool. The inscription at the base reads 'Remember Edward Horton Hubbard, MA, FSA, Architectural Historian 1937–1989'. Designed in antique flash glass it contains 12 small diamond-shaped panes, which will gradually be inscribed as memorials to poets and writers. The abstract design is loosely based on the 13th-century geometrical layout of interrelated roundels. Four authors have so far been commemorated:

Alexander Pope (1688–1744), poet and satirist, author of *An Essay on Man*. The quote "And Heav'n is won by violence of song" is from his *Epistle to Augustus*. **Robert Herrick** (1591–1674), lyric poet. His lines "Gather ye rosebuds while ye may" appear with his name and date. **Oscar Wilde** (1854–1900), playwright. His panel, with just his name and dates but no quote, was added in 1995, the centenary of the first performance of *The Importance of Being Earnest*. **Alfred Edward Housman** (1859–1936), poet and classical scholar. His memorial was added in 1996 to mark the centenary of the publication of *A Shropshire Lad*. (Again, no quote is given). Two further lozenges, commemorating **Frances (Fanny) Burney**, Mme d'Arblay (1752–1840), novelist, and **Christopher Marlowe** (1564–1593), dramatist, will be unveiled during 2002. None of those named in the window are actually buried in the Abbey.

20 BIBLICAL POETS
Designed by Clayton and Bell ◆ Given in 1869

A small window in the east aisle of this transept was given by Dr Nathaniel Rogers, who lived in Westminster, to represent the poets of the Old and New Testaments, King David and St John. The coat of arms assigned to St Edward the Confessor also appears.

21 FRAGMENTS IN EAST CLOISTER

The remains of glass from war-damaged windows were set in an abstract pattern in the half-windows at the north end of this cloister by Goddard and Gibbs in the 1950s. Most of the glass appears to be from the 19th and 20th centuries but there are Tudor quarries at the base of the designs salvaged from the eastern window of Henry VII's Chapel with the initials H and R crowned.

22 JAMES RUSSELL LOWELL (1818–1891)

Designed by Clayton and Bell ◆ Unveiled 28 November 1893

In the vestibule of the Chapter House are four lancet windows in memory of Lowell, poet and United States minister in London. The windows and the tablet below were given by his English friends. The main figures in the triple light are St Botolph, patron saint of Boston (Lowell's native city), Sir Launfal (an armed knight about whom Lowell wrote a poem), and St Ambrose. Below are scenes showing the Pilgrim Fathers with the *Mayflower* in the background, St Martin on his horse beside a beggar, and the emancipation of slaves. The coats of arms held by angels in the single light are those of the USA, *Harvard Graduates Magazine* (a mistake, as they should show the University arms), the Royal arms and the Abbey arms.

**FACING PAGE
Chapter House**

23 CHAPTER HOUSE

Designed by Clayton and Bell (1882) and Joan Howson (1950)

The windows here are a mixture of late 19th- and mid- 20th-century glass, much having been destroyed during the last war. In 1950 panels which survived were incorporated into the present scheme. The window over the entrance, showing Queen Victoria at the top with Elizabeth I, James I, Charles I and William III below, was undamaged. Panels depict scenes from the history of England and the Abbey, with individual figures and coats of arms of kings, abbots, churchmen and benefactors to the Abbey. The older glass can easily be distinguished as each is a square panel depicting a seated figure or scene and the modern glass shows coats of arms. Small designs in the clear glass include representations of air raids and other Second World War operations. Modern inscriptions under each window give a history of this room and its use through the centuries.

24 ROBINSON DUCKWORTH
(1834–1911)

Designed by Francis Skeat

◆ **Unveiled 9 May 1988**

The subject of this small round window opposite the entrance to the Abbey Museum is St Francis and the birds and was designed by Francis Skeat in honour of his great uncle. Robinson Duckworth, Sub-Dean, is buried in the choir of the Abbey and was a close friend of Lewis Carroll. He helped to row Alice Liddell and her sisters in the boat in which the original story of *Alice's Adventures in Wonderland* was told. The design came from Duckworth's bookplate and his arms appear in the window with his motto, translated as Constancy.

25 13TH CENTURY GLASS IN THE MUSEUM

The six panels of 13th-century glass depict the massacre of the Innocents, the Ascension, the descent of the Holy Spirit, the stoning of St Stephen, the beheading of a martyr, and an episode from the life of St Nicholas. Their original position in Henry III's church is not known, but they were displayed for many years in the Jerusalem Chamber before being moved to the Museum in 1987, when they were re-leaded. (A seventh panel of the Resurrection in a very patched condition was moved in the 1950s to the Muniment Room.) An inscription scratched on the Innocents panel reads "Thomas Medbury glassed this 1683", when repairs were obviously made. The Ascension shows the figure of the Virgin Mary in the centre and the Apostles grouped on either side gazing upwards, with only the feet and lower part of the robe of the ascending Christ shown. In the lower part of

the descent of the Holy Spirit panel are shown Our Lady and the Apostles receiving the gifts of the Spirit on the day of Pentecost. The third Person of the Blessed Trinity is symbolised by a descending dove, from which radiates "tongues of fire". The martyr in the beheading scene is most probably St John the Baptist but his head is a modern restoration. The oval panel illustrating the legend of St Nicholas of Myra tells of the saving by the saint of a boy who fell from a ship, with a gold cup in his hand. Due to various repairs it is now difficult to make out all the figures, although the ship, with the boy's father and the sailors on board are quite clear.

South Side, from the east

26 YOUNG MEN'S CHRISTIAN ASSOCIATION 1914–1918
Designed by Dudley Forsyth ◆ Dedicated 14 November 1921

This window records the services rendered during the First World War by the YMCA and commemorates its founder Sir George Williams (1821–1905). There are two small portrait heads of Sir George in youth and old age at the base. The main figures are of St Michael and St George, the patron saint of England, with scenes from the Transfiguration and the Sermon on the Mount below. Niches contain small figures of soldiers from all over the world who served with the British forces, with coats of arms of their countries. At the base is the YMCA symbol and the *chi-rho* sign (the two letters which begin the Greek word for Christ). The inscription reads: 'To the glory of God and in memory of the service rendered through the Young Men's Christian Association during the First World War: and of George Williams, its founder'.

27 ISAMBARD KINGDOM BRUNEL (1806–1859)
Designed by Norman Shaw (1831–1912) ◆ Installed 1868

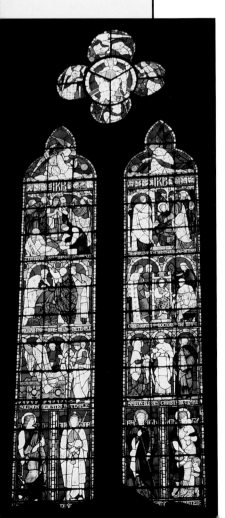

This window to the famous designer of the Clifton Suspension Bridge at Bristol and engineer of the Great Western Railway and the *Great Eastern* steamship is the only one in the Abbey to exhibit a pre-Raphaelite influence. It depicts Biblical scenes concerned with the building of the Temple and Christ's teaching there, (left) Zerubbabel builds the Second Temple, Hilkiah finds the Book of the Law in the Temple and Solomon dedicates the Temple, (right) the disciples show Christ the buildings of the Temple, Christ sits with the doctors in the Temple and Simeon blesses Christ. The figures below these scenes represent Fortitude, Justice, Faith and Charity. In the quatrefoil at the top Christ is shown in Glory. The initials IKB appear at the head of each light but the inscription at the base is obscured by monuments on the window sill. It reads: 'In memory Isambard Kingdom Brunel. Born April 9th 1806: Departed this life September 15th 1859'. The figure subjects were drawn by Henry Holiday and the glass is by Messrs Heaton, Butler and Bayne. It was erected by the Brunel family, originally on the other side of the nave. The window was re-erected in this position in 1952 and several horizontal panels of lilies and pomegranates at the base of the scenes were removed so that the lower figures could be moved up to be seen more clearly.

28 ROYAL FLYING CORPS 1914–18
Designed by Harry Grylls ◆ Dedicated 26 May 1922

Mrs Louis Bennett of West Virginia gave this window in memory of all those of the RFC who died in the First World War. Her son Louis served with the Corps and was killed in France. The inspiration for a window came to Mrs Bennett at the service in the Abbey on October 17 1921 when General Pershing conferred the United

States Congressional Medal of Honor on the British Unknown Warrior. She said in a letter to the Dean "I can hardly grasp the fact that I will be able to add something beautiful to it [the Abbey]. It will comfort me greatly". She chose this position so that through the window "the sunlight falls on the grave of the Unknown Warrior". The theme is flying men and wings, and contains quotes held by the prophets Isaiah and Ezekiel ("They that wait upon the Lord shall renew their strength, they shall mount up with wings as eagles" and "I heard also the noise of the wings of the living creatures as they touched one another".) At the top is a figure of St Michael, patron saint of airmen, trampling on the devil angel. Four larger angels in the main design hold the breastplate of Righteousness, the sword of the Spirit, the helmet of Salvation and the shield of Faith. The face of the angel holding the shield is a portrait of Louis Bennett. The inscription reads: "To the Glory of God and in proud and thankful memory of those members of the British Flying Corps who fell in the Great War 1914–1918". The badge and motto of the RFC (RAF) and that of the West Virginia Flying Corps, incorporating the seal of that State, also appear.

29 GEORGE HERBERT (1593–1633) AND WILLIAM COWPER (1731–1800)
Designed by Clayton and Bell ◆ Given in 1876

These two religious poets both attended Westminster School. This window in St George's chapel was given by George Childs of Philadelphia, USA. The angel in the quatrefoil at the top is flanked by the coats of arms attributed to Herbert and Cowper. Figures of both poets appear below with quotes from their works. From Herbert: "Look not on pleasures as they come but go defer not the least virtue, play the man. If thou do ill the joy fades not the pain, if well the pain doth fade the joy remains". The quote from Cowper comes from On the Receipt of My Mother's Picture: "O that those lips had language. Life has passed with me but roughly since I heard thee last. Voice only fails else how distinct they say 'Grieve not my child, chase all thy fears away".

30 FIGURE OF THE 'BLACK PRINCE'

The single light in St George's Chapel contains fragments of 15th-century glass and has been presumed, since at least the 17th century, to be a figure of Edward the 'Black Prince', son of Edward III. He is clothed in plate armour with a lance in his right hand, a long sword by his side, and wears a surcoat with the arms of France and England quarterly. At his feet is the cross and five martlets assigned to Edward the Confessor, and a red rose of Lancaster. The face of the figure, which was not made from old glass, was replaced when it was repaired by Goddard and Gibbs in the 1950s. The Black Prince has a fine tomb in Canterbury Cathedral.

OPPOSITE TOP Detail of YMCA window

OPPOSITE BOTTOM Brunel's window

ABOVE Detail from the RFC window

31 GREAT WEST WINDOW
Designed by Sir James Thornhill
◆ **Installed 1735**

The design for the Great West window was probably sketched out by Thornhill just before his death, and executed by William Price (son of Joshua), who received £400 towards the work. It shows the figures of Abraham, Isaac and Jacob at the top, with the date 1735. The representatives of the twelve Tribes of Israel are in the two rows below, with the names under each figure ie. Reuben, Simeon, Levi, Judah, Zebulon, Issachar, and Dan and below them Gad, Asher, Naphtali, Joseph, Benjamin, Moses and Aaron. At the base are the coats of arms of (from the left): King Sebert, Queen Elizabeth I, King George II, Joseph Wilcocks (Dean of Westminster), and the City of Westminster. The inscription on the stonework underneath the window records the fact that the west towers were completed in George II's reign (commenced in 1735 and finished by 1745).

32 FIGURE THOUGHT TO BE EDWARD THE CONFESSOR

The head of this rather jumbled figure beneath the north-west tower is thought to be late 14th century but it is not really known who he is meant to represent. He wears a bright crimson robe with a blue mantle. Above his head is a double triangle, the ancient symbol of the Trinity, and the golden crowned portcullis at his feet is Tudor work.

33 RICHARD TREVITHICK (1771–1833)
Designed by Burlison and Grylls
◆ **Installed 1888**

Presented by the Institution of Civil Engineers, the window commemorates this famous Cornish engineer. In the top quatrefoil is St Michael, with angels playing musical instruments. Included in the design are figures of nine Cornish saints (Piran, Petroc, Pinnock, Germanus, Julian, Cyriacus, Constantin, Nonna and Geraint). The face of St Piran is thought to be a portrait of Trevithick. Angels at the base of the window hold scrolls with outline drawings of some of Trevithick's designs and inventions: his tramroad locomotive of 1803, Cornish pumping engine, steam dredger and railway locomotive of 1808. The inscription

reads: 'Richard Trevithick born 13 April 1771 died 22 April 1833'. The window was moved from its original position in the second bay in order to accommodate the Comper series.

34 SIR HENRY ROYCE (1863–1933)
Designed by J.Ninian Comper ◆ **Unveiled 23 October 1962**

This depicts eight-foot high figures of King Edgar (first king of all England who died in AD 975) and St Dunstan. In the quatrefoil the scene shows Edgar sailing into Chester with six kings with whom he had made peace. The scene is flanked by the coats of arms of the sees of London, Canterbury and Worcester. St Dunstan (d.988) was Bishop of London and Worcester and Archbishop of Canterbury. He brought Benedictine monks to Westminster in about AD 960. Above the figure of the King is a representation, taken from a pen drawing by Dunstan himself, of Our Lord enthroned and the Saint kneeling before Him. The other scene shows St Dunstan reading, when his harp, hung on the wall of his cell, was played by an angel. The coat of arms with a cross and four martlets (birds) attributed to Edgar and the cross of St George appear beside him. Beside Dunstan appear shields showing a ciborium (covered cup), two mitres and crossed croziers (representing his two bishoprics), and the cross on a green field with the seated Virgin representing Glastonbury where Dunstan was Abbot. Royce, with his partner Charles Rolls, designed the world famous Rolls-Royce motor cars, and also aero engines, including that which won the Schneider Trophy in the 1930s (the forerunner of the engine which powered the wartime 'Spitfire'). Sir Henry's arms, and

FAR LEFT The Great West window

LEFT Detail from the Great West window

ABOVE Angels in the Trevithick window

those of the City of Derby where his cars were made, are shown at the base. Although this window begins the series of windows by Comper, it was actually the last one to be unveiled. The inscription reads: "In memory of Frederick Henry Royce O.B.E. Baronet, Engineer. Born 1863. Died 1933".

35 THE ROYAL ARMY MEDICAL CORPS
Designed by J.Ninian Comper ◆ Unveiled 22 May 1927

Figures of St Edward the Confessor (d.1066) and Abbot Edwin appear here. The arms attributed to St Edward (a cross and five martlets) appear in the quatrefoil. Above Edward's figure is a scene showing him 'touching for the king's evil' and the corresponding scene shows him giving his ring as alms to St John the Evangelist, who is disguised as a poor pilgrim. He also holds the ring in the main picture and from his wrist hang tablets inscribed with the opening words of his charter to the Abbey. The Abbot is in his Benedictine habit (black being shown as blue in stained glass) holding his crozier but without the mitre and ring which belong to a later period. The red shield with the keys of St Peter and ring of St Edward as well as the ancient shield of the Abbey also appear. The window is in memory of all those in the RAMC who died in the 1914–18 war. The inscription at the base was altered to include those who also died serving in the 1939–45 war and now reads:

'In memory of the Royal Army Medical Corps of all ranks who gave their lives in the service of their country'. The badge and motto of the Corps appear at the bottom of each light, between the Royal arms and Union Flag. Rolls of Honour for the RAMC are displayed in the Chapter House.

36 SIR CHARLES PARSONS (1854–1931)
Designed by J.Ninian Comper ◆ Unveiled 5 October 1950

Scientist and marine engineer who developed the steam turbine, he has been called the greatest steam engineer since James Watt. The figures here are

LEFT The Royce memorial window

RIGHT St Edward from the RAMC window

FAR RIGHT The Wolfe-Barry window

King Henry III (d.1272), who built most of the present Abbey, and Abbot Richard de Ware. At the top are the arms of Henry dimidiating those of his wife Eleanor of Provence, flanked by the lion of Simon de Montfort, St Hugh of Lincoln and the ancient shield of France. The King's figure is based on his tomb effigy in St Edward's Chapel and he holds a model of the apse of the Abbey. Above him angels hold a shield with the three lions of England. The other coats of arms shown are those of Provence and England dimidiating Angoulême, where his mother came from. The Abbot was the author of the *Customary* or rules for the daily life of the monastery and the great Cosmati pavement was laid in front of the High Altar in his time (1268). Here Comper made a slight mistake as Ware is shown wearing a pallium to which he was never entitled as he was not an archbishop. He is flanked by the arms of the Confessor and the monastery of Westminster with the addition of the mitre and crozier. At the bottom of the window are the heraldic achievements of Parsons and the City of Newcastle upon Tyne. The inscription reads: "In memory of Charles Algernon Parsons O.M., K.C.B., F.R.S. Marine Engineer. Born Anno Dni. 1854. Died Anno Dni. 1931".

37 SIR JOHN WOLFE-BARRY (1836–1918)
Designed by J.Ninian Comper
◆ **Unveiled 7 December 1922**

Sir John designed many London bridges including Blackfriars Bridge and Tower Bridge and he also worked on sections of the London Underground system. He was the son of Sir Charles Barry who designed the Palace of Westminster. The large figures are of King Edward I (d.1307) and Abbot Walter de Wenlok. The shield of England appears at the top with the Welsh dragon and Scottish lion. The shield of Jerusalem has reference to the King as a Crusader. In the scene above the King is the Coronation Chair containing the Stone of Destiny which he brought to the Abbey from Scone in Scotland. A sleeping figure recalls the legend that the patriarch Jacob used the stone for a pillow when he saw his vision of angels ascending and descending on the ladder from Heaven. The small statuettes above this scene are figures of Eleanor of Castile, the king's wife. Both are buried in St Edward's Chapel. The other shields show the quartered arms of Castile and Leon and the arms of Ponthieu. His badge of the golden rose and motto 'Keep Troth' appear in the borders with statuettes of his ten children and others. The scene above the Abbot shows him riding with two monks and the statuettes represent him giving the heart of Henry III to the Abbess of Fontevrault for burial there. The inscription reads: "In memory of John Wolfe Barry, K.C.B., F.R.S. Civil Engineer. Born 1836. Died 1918". Below this, rather obscured by monuments on the window sill, are various shields connected with Sir John as well as his own personal arms. J.Ninian Comper, who was knighted in 1950, is buried just in front of this window.

38 SIR BENJAMIN BAKER (1840–1907)

Designed by J.Ninian Comper ◆ Unveiled 3 December 1909

Engineer of the Forth Bridge in Scotland and the Assouan Dam in Egypt. He also worked on parts of the London 'tube' network. The large figures are of King Edward III (d.1377) and Simon de Langham, the only abbot of Westminster to be made a cardinal. In the quatrefoil at the very top is St George fighting the dragon. The small statuettes in the borders represent the children of the King with their own coats of arms or those of their father, below each one. Langham holds a plan of the nave, the re-building of which was largely due to his generosity. Behind him are the arms of the sees of Canterbury and Ely (three crowns) and in the scene above angels hold his own coat of arms (a gold shield with a red chevron and three green triple-petalled plants).

The window was presented to the Dean and Chapter by the Earl of Cromer on behalf of the Institution of Civil Engineers. The inscription reads: "In memory of Sir Benjamin Baker, Civil Engineer. Forth Bridge. Assouan Dam. B.1840. D.1907".

39 DONALD ALEXANDER SMITH, BARON STRATHCONA (1820–1914)

Designed by J.Ninian Comper ◆ Unveiled 1 July 1919

Smith emigrated from Scotland to Canada, served in the Hudson Bay Company and helped build the Canadian Pacific Railway. He became High Commissioner for Canada in London and was raised to the peerage as Lord Strathcona in 1897. The figures show King Richard II (d.1400) and Abbot Nicholas Litlyngton. Richard II was devoted to St Edward the Confessor and gave money towards the building of the nave. His figure is based on the contemporary painted portrait which hangs in the nave and on his gilt bronze tomb effigy. Above him is a scene showing him riding out after the death of Wat Tyler, leader of the 'Peasants' Revolt' and addressing the rebels while the scene opposite shows him hearing mass in